FOOD MATTERS

GLUTEN-FREE
AND OTHER SPECIAL DIETS

by Marcia Amidon Lusted

Content Consultant
Shahla Ray, PhD
Department of Applied Health Science
Indiana University

Core Library

An Imprint of Abdo Publishing
abdopublishing.com

abdopublishing.com

Published by Abdo Publishing, a division of ABDO, PO Box 398166, Minneapolis, Minnesota 55439. Copyright © 2016 by Abdo Consulting Group, Inc. International copyrights reserved in all countries. No part of this book may be reproduced in any form without written permission from the publisher. Core Library™ is a trademark and logo of Abdo Publishing.

Printed in the United States of America, North Mankato, Minnesota
032015
092015

Cover Photo: Catherine Lane/Getty Images
Interior Photos: Catherine Lane/Getty Images, 1; iStockphoto, 4, 34; Richard B. Levine/Newscom, 7, 32; Shutterstock Images, 9, 16, 28, 41, 45; M.L. Johnson/AP Images, 11; Jon Elswick/AP Images, 12; Red Line Editorial, 18, 30; Ton Koene/VWPics/Newscom, 20; Fred de Noyelle/ Godong/Picture Alliance/Newscom, 23; Igor Dutina/iStock, 26; Justin Sullivan/Getty Images News/Thinkstock, 36; Tim Boyle/Getty Images News/Thinkstock, 39

Editor: Mirella Miller
Series Designer: Becky Daum

Library of Congress Control Number: 2015931578

Cataloging-in-Publication Data
Lusted, Marcia Amidon.
 Gluten-free and other special diets / Marcia Amidon Lusted.
   p. cm. -- (Food matters)
Includes bibliographical references and index.
ISBN 978-1-62403-865-5
1. Wheat-free diet--Juvenile literature.   I. Title.
641.5--dc23
                                                                    2015931578

CONTENTS

CHAPTER ONE

WHAT ARE YOU EATING?

magine your doctor has told you that you cannot eat wheat because it makes you sick. You have already been invited to a friend's birthday party a few days later. You cannot wait to play games and have fun. You are excited to eat hot dogs in buns, chips, candy, and birthday cake. You did not know that many of these foods contain gluten, which is

For someone following a special diet or dealing with a food allergy, it is important to know the ingredients in different foods.

found in grains, such as wheat. What can you eat? What can you not eat?

A gluten-free diet is one of many special diets that can affect day-to-day routine. Learning more about these diets can help you better understand nutrition and identify possible food issues.

Special diets are becoming more common all over the world. A special diet can make a big difference for people with medical conditions, people wanting to lose weight, or people wanting to be healthier. The word "diet" causes most people to think about losing weight. But the word refers to foods a person or

People who cannot or do not eat dairy products can buy items such as lactose-free milk.

community eats regularly, not just to special foods that someone eats or avoids eating to lose weight. People eating gluten-free, dairy-free, or meat-free diets intentionally avoid eating certain kinds of foods.

Doctor's Orders

Scientists and nutritionists create balanced diets. They make sure people take in enough nutrients to stay healthy. These experts know how foods affect the body in different ways. Doctors can use this knowledge, as well as specific medical tests, to determine what foods might be making someone sick. They help people tailor their food choices to deal with illnesses or live healthier lives.

Doctors or dietitians may give their patients information about diets for weight loss, especially for obese people. But there are also diets for people with certain medical conditions. Illnesses such as obesity, diabetes, heart disease, high blood pressure, and high cholesterol are often related to or made worse by what a person eats. Some nutrients that are healthy in small amounts can be harmful in excess. Too much salt, fat, or sugar can be bad for people suffering from one of these conditions.

There are also medical conditions that make eating certain foods dangerous. People with celiac disease have digestive systems that are unable to process wheat. People who are lactose intolerant cannot properly digest the sugar found in milk and

Eating too many foods with high amounts of certain ingredients, such as sugar or salt, can be harmful for some people with health conditions.

most dairy products. These conditions require a complete change in what a person consumes.

In other cases, some people follow special diets because of their religious beliefs or ethical values. Some or all meats are often avoided for these reasons. There are also some people who only eat what they can grow for themselves.

Society is getting better at helping people who follow special diets. Grocery stores are carrying more gluten-free and dairy-free foods and ingredients. Restaurants are more likely to have gluten-free and vegetarian items on their menus. So what exactly are the beliefs behind some of the special diets people follow? Why do people start them, and what can they achieve as a result?

YOUR LIFE
School Food

Does your school serve healthy food? Are there options for kids who do not eat meat or cannot have dairy? What foods fill the school vending machines? Are there soda, candy, and chips? Or are there healthier options, such as water, dried fruit, and nuts? Investigate your school's policies about food, both in the cafeteria menu and the vending machines. Is it possible for you and your classmates to make good food choices at your school?

People who follow special diets are finding it easier to get the foods they need.

CHAPTER TWO

GOING GLUTEN-FREE

One of the most common diets people follow today is a gluten-free diet. Some people adopt this way of eating because they have celiac disease. Following a gluten-free diet helps them control the disease and prevent related problems. However, some people start following a gluten-free diet because they believe it is healthier.

More and more gluten-free foods are becoming available to consumers.

Gluten is a protein commonly found in grains, including wheat, rye, barley, and triticale, which is a cross between wheat and rye. It can be frustrating to follow a gluten-free diet because wheat products are found in many foods. Breads, cakes, cereals, candies, soups, and salad dressings often contain gluten. Some foods that do not contain gluten are contaminated with gluten by coming into contact with wheat at some stage of production. As a result, they end up containing traces, or sometimes larger amounts, of gluten.

YOUR LIFE
Gluten-Free Foods

Gluten-free foods are becoming more common in regular grocery stores. Even traditionally grain-based breads and pastas now offer gluten-free options. This means these products use flour made from brown rice, fava or white beans, potatoes, or oats instead. Find regular pasta and a gluten-free pasta at the grocery store. Then compare the ingredients. What is different between the products? What is the same? Do you notice any other differences?

Celiac Disease

Gluten triggers an immune response in the intestines of a person with celiac disease. White blood cells, the body's infection fighters, attack the small intestine because they recognize a threat to the body. That attack on the small intestine damages the villi, which line the walls of the intestine. Villi help make it possible for the small intestine to absorb nutrients from the foods we eat. If these villi are damaged, then the body is not able to receive nutrients the way it should. This can cause abdominal pain, diarrhea, weight loss, fatigue, and even behavior problems. But some people with celiac disease have no symptoms at all.

There are some negative side effects to avoiding gluten when you do not have celiac disease. Many grains that contain gluten are also good sources of nutrients, including vitamins, minerals, and fiber. People on gluten-free diets have to be very careful that they are still getting the nutrients they need.

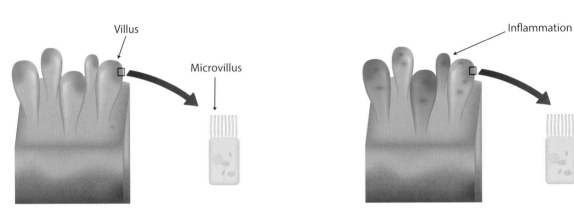

Normal **Celiac Disease**

Villus

Microvillus

Inflammation

Celiac disease causes inflammation in the small intestine if a person eats gluten products.

Paleo Diet

Another diet focused on eating whole, unprocessed foods is the Paleo diet. People who follow the Paleo diet claim these foods are healthier for human bodies, avoiding some of the harmful ingredients that come from processed foods. Some people nickname this the "caveman" diet because early people ate only what they could hunt or gather from wildlife. This name is misleading since modern people eat many things cavemen did not, and no one is exactly sure what early humans ate. People who follow a Paleo diet eat organic foods, including fresh fruits and vegetables, eggs, nuts, and some fats. Organic foods are grown without chemical fertilizers, antibiotics, or modification, in as natural a way as possible. Some Paleo eaters might avoid gluten and carbohydrates completely, while others occasionally eat rice or potatoes. Organic meat that does not contain steroids or antibiotics is also allowed.

Paleolithic Era

The term *Paleo* comes from *Paleolithic*, which refers to the Paleolithic era. This era lasted approximately 2.5 million years and ended 10,000 years ago. During the Paleolithic era, people were hunter-gatherers, meaning they ate only what they could gather from wild plants or from hunting wild animals. The Paleolithic era ended when people began to grow their own crops and raise animals for food.

Enjoy	Avoid
Meats and fish	Grains
Vegetables	Legumes
Fruits	Dairy
Nuts	Processed foods
Seeds	Starches
Healthy fats	Potatoes

Paleo Shopping Cart
This chart shows what kinds of foods are okay to eat on the Paleo diet, as well as foods that cannot be eaten. Why do you think people following the Paleo diet make these food choices?

Cons of the Paleo Diet

Some people disagree with the Paleo diet. They argue that people today are not genetically similar to people who lived during the Paleolithic era. Early people had much shorter lifespans. Critics also point out that there is no way to know what early people ate or how much. Plants change over time as well and do not have the same nutritional qualities they may have had in Paleo times.

Others argue that the Paleo diet is impractical because it can result in higher grocery bills. Someone who is trying to feed a family on whole, unprocessed, organic foods will pay more at the grocery store than someone who buys processed foods. Even though the organic foods are healthier, they may be out of reach economically for many people.

EXPLORE ONLINE

The focus in Chapter Two is on gluten-free and Paleo diets. It also touches on how the Paleo diet may not be healthy. The website below focuses on the Paleo diet. As you know, every source is different. How is the information given in the website different from the information in this chapter? What information is the same? How do the two sources present information differently? What can you learn from this website?

Pros and Cons of the Paleo Diet

mycorelibrary.com/special-diets

EAT YOUR VEGGIES

One of the oldest special diets is vegetarianism. Vegetarians are people who do not eat meat. Most of their food comes from fresh fruits, vegetables, grains, and nuts. There are also very strict vegetarians who do not eat any animal products, including eggs and milk. They are known as vegans.

Vegans eat only products that have not been produced by animals.

Some people follow vegetarianism for religious reasons. These religions have rules against harming or killing animals. People who follow Hinduism do not eat any form of beef because they believe cows are sacred. People who practice Jainism believe it is wrong to kill or harm any living creature, and its followers are expected to be vegetarians. The Taoist religion of China believes nature is sacred, and so vegetarianism is favored. Judaism allows the eating of meat but only if the animals have been killed in a humane manner.

Types of Vegetarianism

Not all vegetarians follow this diet for religious

Animal Rights

For animal rights supporters, not eating meat is a way to protest the treatment of animals that are routinely raised for their meat. Some of these animals live in crowded conditions or are treated harshly. By not buying and eating meat, animal rights supporters are taking a stand against this kind of treatment. Other people may choose to eat only the meat or eggs of animals raised in a more natural environment, such as grass-fed cows and free-range chickens.

Buddhism encourages its followers not to eat meat.

reasons. Many people choose vegetarianism for health reasons too. Some types of vegetarianism are stricter than others. Some people are semivegetarians, meaning they do not eat red meat but will eat chicken and fish. A pescetarian eats only fish. Ovo-vegetarians eat eggs but no milk or dairy products, while lacto-ovo vegetarians eat eggs and all dairy products but no meat. Pollo-vegetarians eat only chicken. There are even flexitarians, who do not stop eating meat but try to eat more fruits, veggies, tofu, lentils, peas, nuts, and seeds. They still eat a steak or a hamburger once in a while. Finally, vegans are the most committed of the vegetarians because they do not eat any meat or any other product that comes from an animal. Some very strict vegans will not even wear clothing made from animals, such as leather.

Receiving Nutrients

It can be difficult to make sure the body is receiving enough nutrients on a vegetarian diet. Nutrients such as iron, calcium, zinc, vitamin D, vitamin B12, and protein are commonly found in meat, milk, and eggs. Dried beans, green leafy vegetables, peas, lentils, and almonds are all important foods for vegetarians to eat. They provide calcium, protein, and other important vitamins and minerals usually found in meat and dairy. Protein can also come from peanut butter, tofu, nuts and seeds, soy milk, and grains. It is important for vegetarians to speak with a doctor or a nutritionist to make sure they have a balanced and healthy diet.

The Good and the Bad

Scientists have found evidence that there are many advantages to eating a vegetarian diet. Vegetarians typically have healthy body weights and lower levels of cholesterol than many nonvegetarians. Vegetarians also live longer on average and have a lower risk of developing cancer and several other diseases.

There is also controversy over vegetarianism. One main argument is whether humans were intended to eat meat. Some people believe humans' brains

Tofu and soybeans are just two of the foods vegetarians can eat for protein.

developed over time in order to eat meat for the protein and other nutrients they needed to be healthy.

Hinduism strongly encourages vegetarianism and prohibits killing and eating cows. The following excerpt is from the Hindu text *The Law of Manu*, from approximately 1500 BCE:

> *Meat cannot be obtained without injury to animals, and the slaughter of animals obstructs the way to Heaven; let him therefore shun the use of meat. . . . He who does not eat meat becomes dear to men, and will not be tormented by diseases. He who permits the slaughter of an animal, he who kills it, he who cuts it up, he who buys or sells meat, he who cooks it, he who serves it up, and he who eats it, are all slayers. There is no greater sinner than that man who seeks to increase the bulk of his own flesh by the flesh of other beings. . . . Thus having well considered the disgusting origin of meat and the cruelty of fettering and slaying of corporeal beings, let him entirely abstain from eating flesh.*

Source: "The World History of Animal Rights and Vegetarianism in Quotes." All Creation Liberation. Reverend Rebecca, n.d. Web. Accessed December 5, 2014.

What's the Big Idea?

Take a close look at this passage. What is the main connection being made between Hinduism and whether animals should be eaten? What can you tell about the Hindu's relationship with living creatures according to this excerpt? Does it go beyond simply talking about animals and food?

CHAPTER FOUR

DAIRY-FREE DIETS

M any vegetarians choose not to drink milk or eat dairy products. But there are people who cannot have dairy because of a medical condition known as lactose intolerance. Lactose is a sugar found in dairy products. People with lactose intolerance are unable to fully digest milk sugar.

When people take in lactose, an enzyme known as lactase attaches itself to the lactose in the small

Soy milk, almond milk, and rice milk are some alternatives for people who cannot have dairy.

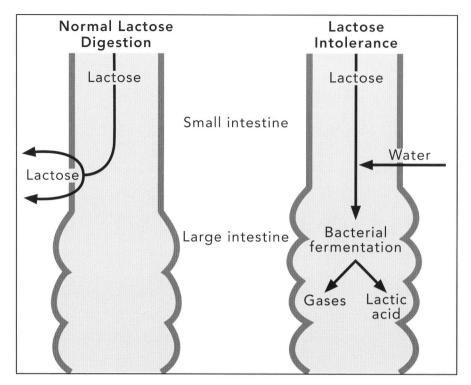

Lactose Intolerance

Just what does lactose intolerance do to the digestive system? This diagram shows the difference between healthy lactose digestion and lactose intolerance. After reading this chapter, what kinds of symptoms can lactose intolerance cause? What foods should people with lactose intolerance stay away from?

intestine. The enzyme breaks down lactose into two simple sugars that are easy for the body to absorb. People with lactose intolerance do not have enough lactase in their intestines. The lactose they ingest moves into the colon without being processed, creating the symptoms of lactose intolerance. Many people actually have low levels of lactase, but only some people have lactose intolerance symptoms. These can include nausea, cramps, vomiting, diarrhea, bloating, and gas. Usually these symptoms are mild, but in some people they can be severe.

Causes of Lactose Intolerance

Sometimes lactose intolerance happens because of aging. The human body produces large amounts of lactase at birth and during early childhood, when we drink the most milk. As the diet becomes more varied and the body consumes less milk, lactase production

Family Tree

Certain ethnic groups are more likely to suffer from lactose intolerance because their ancestors' diets did not include as many dairy products. Their ancestors' bodies did not learn to digest it, and they passed this intolerance from generation to generation. Most Asians and Native Americans are lactose intolerant, and many Africans and Hispanics have some symptoms of lactose intolerance.

Probiotics are often available in yogurt or as capsules.

decreases. Another cause of lactose intolerance is illness or injury to the small intestine. This can happen because of surgery or intestinal diseases. Some babies are born with lactose intolerance, and it is usually something they inherit from a parent. These babies have to drink infant formula that does not contain lactose.

The Lactose-Intolerance Diet

People who have lactose intolerance may have it only mildly. Often they can control it with medication or by limiting how much dairy they eat. They may also eat foods that contain probiotics, which are living organisms found in the intestines that help maintain healthy digestion.

People with more severe lactose intolerance must make bigger adjustments to their diets by not eating any dairy at all. This is difficult because lactose is found in many foods where you might not expect to find it, such as cereal, instant soup, salad dressing, processed meat, and baking mixes. There are also special foods made for people with lactose intolerance. Some dairy foods, such as Swiss or cheddar cheese and yogurt, have very

YOUR LIFE
Be a Lactose Detective

If you have symptoms of lactose intolerance, it is important to learn how to read the labels on food before you buy it. If the list of ingredients includes milk, milk solids, nonfat milk solids, milk powder, lactose, casein, whey, or cream, then you want to avoid eating those products, or eat them only in very small amounts.

It can be difficult to follow a lactose-intolerance diet, since many popular foods such as ice cream, pizza, and milk shakes contain lactose.

small amounts of lactose and do not generally cause symptoms.

Unlike some special diets, a lactose-intolerance diet is a treatment for a specific medical condition and is not adopted due to lifestyle or healthy eating concerns. But following it can improve the quality of life for someone who suffers from lactose intolerance.

While most scientists agree that calcium is necessary for health, it does not have to come from one source. According to the Harvard University School of Public Health:

> *The pro-milk faction believes that increased calcium intake—particularly in the form of the currently recommended three glasses of milk per day—will help prevent osteoporosis, the weakening of bones.*
>
> *On the other side are those who believe that consuming a lot of milk and other dairy products . . . may contribute to problems such as heart disease or prostate cancer. . . .*
>
> *For individuals who are unable to digest—or who dislike— dairy products. . . .Calcium can also be found in dark green, leafy vegetables, such as kale and collard greens, as well as in dried beans and legumes.*

Source: "Calcium and Milk: What's Best for Your Bones and Health?" Harvard School of Public Health. *Harvard College, n.d. Web. Accessed December 5, 2014.*

Changing Minds

Decide your position on drinking milk. Research both sides of the issue. Now imagine that your parents have the opposite opinion. Write them a letter in which you explain why you do or do not believe you should be drinking milk and why. Be sure to include facts and details to support your opinion.

CHAPTER FIVE

HERE TODAY, GONE TOMORROW

People follow special diets because of medical conditions or because they want to be healthier. There are many good, established diets that help people accomplish these goals. But many people follow a diet just to lose weight. The weight loss industry is large and makes a lot of money from people seeking quick and easy diet plans. This category of diets is called fad diets.

The Atkins Diet is one example of a fad diet.

A fad diet promises dramatic results quickly. These diets get publicity from books, television shows, websites, and celebrity endorsements. Companies try to convince people to try their diets by claiming they are new and effective. Many fad diets use special pills, powders, and herbs. Others make you stop eating fat, sugar, or carbohydrates. Some fad diets also require skipping meals or drastically reducing the number of calories. Fad diets usually do not cause long-term weight loss and can even be seriously unhealthy.

Water, Water Everywhere

Many fad diets work right away because they encourage the body to shed water. This is the body's first response to being given fewer calories from food. At first, this loss of water may result in losing 2 to 3 pounds (1 to 1.4 kg) in a week. But as soon as the body begins eating normally again, the water weight will come back.

A Menu of Fad Diets

For decades, people have tried different fad diets in order to lose weight, feel more attractive, or correct a medical problem. Some

Some stores cater to fad diets or low-carb diets.

of these diets have been around for a long time. The South Beach Diet focuses on protein, low fat dairy, whole grains, vegetables, and fruits. Other diets focus on foods from countries, such as Greece and Italy. These heart-healthy foods include seafood, nuts, fruits, and olive oil.

The Atkins Diet limits the amount of heavily processed flour and sugar and suggests eating protein. But this diet is not well balanced and lacks a healthy amount of calcium.

Eating a healthy diet means paying attention to the food on your plate. People with gluten and lactose intolerances must remove foods from their diets that can cause problems. Following other special diets also requires work. Science continues to discover new information about how food can affect health and medical conditions. Learning about special diets and healthy eating helps people make good choices for a healthy body and mind.

YOUR LIFE
Making Good Choices

If you feel like you are having problems with certain foods, such as dairy or gluten, or you want to eat a healthier diet, it is important to talk to your parents and your doctor. They can help determine if you have a food intolerance or allergy. They can also help you create an eating plan that gives your growing body the nutrition it needs while still helping you eat better or differently.

It is important to eat a balanced diet with enough nutrients, no matter your food allergies or beliefs.

FURTHER EVIDENCE

There is quite a bit of information about fad diets in Chapter Five. It also covers the risks of fad diets. What is the main point of this chapter? What key evidence supports this point? Go to the article on fad diets at the website below. Find a quote from the website that supports the chapter's main point. Does the quote support an existing piece of evidence in the chapter? Or does it add a new one?

The Deal with Diets
mycorelibrary.com/special-diets

Gluten-Free Diets

- Gluten is a protein found in grains that irritates the small intestine of people who have celiac disease.

Vegetarians

- There are many types of vegetarians, including those who eat some meat, those who eat no meat but some dairy, and those who eat no animal products at all.

Lactose Intolerance

- People without enough lactase in their digestive system cannot properly digest lactose, which can lead to stomach problems.

Fad Diets

- Fad diets often promote fast weight loss but not long-term health. Many fad diets are unhealthy or even dangerous.

A Paleo Snack

You can make your own Paleo trail mix by combining any of the following ingredients. Be sure all the ingredients are unsweetened and have not been treated with sulfur dioxide to prevent browning and preserve freshness.

- Sunflower seeds
- Macadamia nuts
- Coconut flakes
- Almonds
- Dried blueberries
- Banana chips
- Pistachios
- Walnuts
- Dried apricots or cherries
- Dried pineapple
- Chopped dry dates
- Raisins

Choose the ingredients that sound good to you, combine, and snack!

Why Do I Care?

Maybe you do not have health issues. But that doesn't mean you can't think about healthier ways to eat. How do special diets affect your life? Do you have friends or family who follow special diets? How might your life be different if you had an allergy?

You Are There

This book discusses how it can be hard to make food choices in schools when you follow a special diet. Imagine you get to decide your school lunch menu every day. After reading about these different diets, dietary needs, and ideas about proper nutrition, what changes would you make to the menu? Would you have more options? How would the students and parents feel about the changes?

Take a Stand

This book discusses the Paleo diet. Do you think this is a good diet to follow? Or do you think the arguments people make for eating this way are strong enough? Write a short essay explaining your opinion. Make sure to give reasons for your opinion and facts and details that support those reasons.

Say What?

Studying diets and nutrition can mean learning a lot of new vocabulary. Find five words in this book that you've never heard before. Use a dictionary to find out what they mean. Then write their meanings in your own words, and use each new word in a sentence.

GLOSSARY

antibiotics
drugs that are used to kill bacteria

carbohydrates
various substances found in foods that are made of carbon, hydrogen, and oxygen

enzyme
a protein in human cells that is capable of producing chemical changes, such as digestion

fertilizers
substances that are added to soil and help plants grow

herbicides
chemicals used to kill unwanted plants, such as weeds

lactose
a kind of sugar found in milk

nutrients
things that nourish, especially in food

pesticides
chemicals used to kill harmful insects

prescribe
to officially advise someone to use something as a treatment

LEARN MORE

Books

Bryan, Dale-Marie. *Living with Celiac Disease.* Minneapolis: Abdo Publishing, 2012.

Nardo, Don. *Vegan Diets.* Farmington Hills, MI: Greenhaven Press, 2013.

Petrie, Kristin. *Food Options: Following Special Diets.* Minneapolis: Abdo Publishing, 2012.

Websites

To learn more about Food Matters, visit **booklinks.abdopublishing.com**. These links are routinely monitored and updated to provide the most current information available.

Visit **mycorelibrary.com** for free additional tools for teachers and students.

INDEX

ABOUT THE AUTHOR

Marcia Amidon Lusted is the author of more than 95 books for young readers and hundreds of magazine articles. She is also the editor of *AppleSeeds* magazine, a writing instructor, and a musician. She lives in New Hampshire.